Contents

What is coming of age?

*T*he expression 'coming of age' can mean many things. Some people use it to describe the time when a young person begins to think independently and responsibly. In some cultures, when a person comes of age he or she is given a responsible role in the community. This often marks the beginning of independence from the family.

In some cultures, this rite of passage is an important and symbolic event because it celebrates the role of a young adult in the community. In other cultures, the rite of passage is simply a reason for a party. Sometimes the rite is based on religious beliefs, symbolizing the time when a young person makes an independent choice to commit to a particular religion.

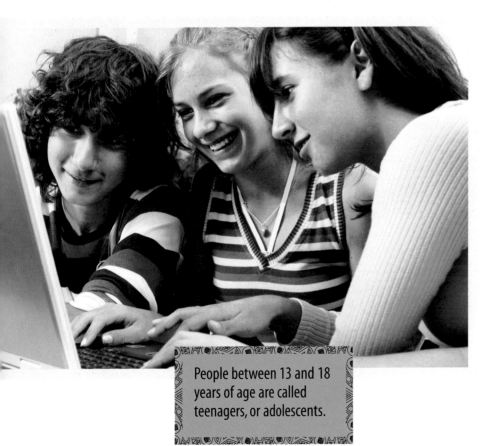

People between 13 and 18 years of age are called teenagers, or adolescents.

Coming of age rites are often held between childhood and adulthood. This time is known as adolescence. It is when both boys and girls experience puberty, as their bodies gradually develop into those of young adults. Both sexes also experience many emotional changes, as they come to terms with their changing bodies and try to find a sense of identity as young adults. In many cultures young people are said to come of age during adolescence.

The film *Ferris Bueller's Day Off* tells the story of how one young man comes of age.

The age at which a person is legally an adult varies across the world. In law, when a person is an adult he or she can vote, drink alcohol (in some countries) and marry. An adult also has to take responsibility for his or her behaviour. Some coming of age rites reflect the legal age of adulthood.

A genre (type) of film called a 'coming of age' movie usually tells the story of an individual during the transition from childhood to young adulthood. The film follows the young person as he or she experiences, learns and takes on responsibility as an adult.

This book looks at how six major religions mark a person's coming of age. It covers the preparation, and the ceremony and its significance within the religion for the individual and community. It also looks at ways in which other societies and cultures mark this rite of passage.

FOCUS ON:
Ancient Rome

In Ancient Rome, a boy came of age on his 16th birthday. At this time, he gave up wearing his childhood lucky charm called a *bulla*. He began to wear men's clothes instead of the white toga (tunic) worn by children. He was then considered a man. At 14, girls were expected to give up their toys. They could marry and start a family.

Marking coming of age

*A*cross the world there are several different branches of the Christian Church. The main branches are Roman Catholic, Orthodox and Protestant, but within those there are many denominations. Most Christian denominations share the same core beliefs but emphasize different aspects of belief. This is reflected in the different ways in which they mark a person's coming of age.

Many Christians mark an individual's coming of age with a ceremony and service called *confirmation*. This confirms or strengthens a person's commitment to Christianity. Christians usually baptize or christen their babies. At baptism, the baby's parents and godparents promise to bring up the child in a Christian way, and to offer Christian guidance and support. At confirmation, a boy or girl makes an independent choice to honour the promises that were made on their behalf at baptism. Anyone who has been baptized and has taken part in the necessary preparations can be confirmed.

In the Orthodox Churches, babies are confirmed immediately after baptism in a ceremony called *chrismation*. In the Roman Catholic Church, confirmation usually happens when a child is about eight. Many Protestant denominations confirm people in their early teens.

Many Protestant people are confirmed as adolescents, by which time the Church believes they are mature enough to take part in this important rite of passage.

In the past, people who were preparing for confirmation had to learn off by heart some of the most important Christian teachings. These included the Apostles' Creed, the Ten Commandments and the Lord's Prayer. They also had to learn a series of set questions and answers summarizing the Christian faith. This is called the *catechism*.

Many Christians still learn these today, but most churches also hold courses to prepare young people for confirmation. The courses concentrate on discussing what it means to be a Christian, and to deepen one's relationship with God.

Confirmation usually takes place in the family's local church or cathedral, but sometimes a group of children is confirmed at their school, if it is a church school. There are no rules about what to wear, but most people dress smartly.

Some Christians believe that confirmation is a sacrament. This is an experience when Christians believe they are receiving special blessings from God.

These Roman Catholic children are dressed for their confirmation ceremony. Children are often confirmed in large groups by a bishop during Mass, the Roman Catholic church service.

FOCUS ON:
The Trinity

Christians believe in the Trinity – that God is three persons: God the Father, the spirit and eternal loving creator; Christ the Son, the perfect manifestation of God in human form; and the Holy Spirit who is the power of God working in the world. Christians believe that Jesus Christ rose from death after crucifixion (when he was killed on the cross). After this, the Holy Spirit was sent to Christ's disciples or followers to give them the power to preach about Christ. The gifts of the Holy Spirit (see page 11), which a newly-confirmed Christian receives, are an important part of Christian belief.

The confirmation ceremony

Each person taking confirmation has a sponsor, who acts as a guide in their faith. The sponsor is usually a friend and a practising Christian. Sponsors must have been confirmed themselves, to show their commitment to God and the church. They must also be at least 16 years old.

At infant baptisms, a baby is given a name, which is chosen by the parents. In Roman Catholic Churches, confirmation is an opportunity for the individual to choose an additional name. People usually choose the name of a saint who they may have studied during confirmation classes and who they find particularly inspiring. The bishop uses this confirmation name during the service.

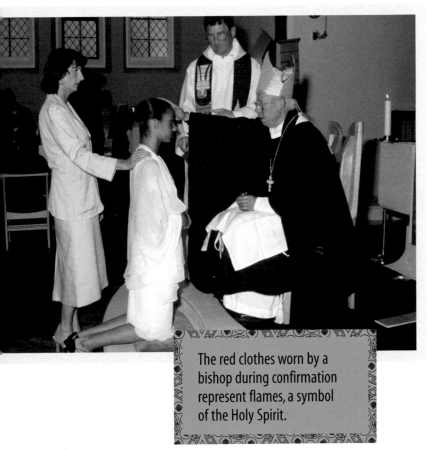

The red clothes worn by a bishop during confirmation represent flames, a symbol of the Holy Spirit.

Dressed in red robes, a bishop usually leads the service. The bishop asks the confirmation candidates questions about their faith and commitment. The candidates promise to reject evil, then renew the promises made on their behalf at baptism. The bishop leads a prayer asking God to strengthen those who are confirmed with the Holy Spirit. The bishop places his hands on the head of the person being confirmed, saying, 'Defend, O Lord, this child with your heavenly grace, that he may continue yours for ever; and daily increase in your Holy Spirit, more and more, until he comes into your everlasting kingdom.' For some Christians, the laying on of the hands is a very important moment, because it is when they receive the Holy Spirit.

Everyone in the church, called the congregation, then recites the Apostles' Creed. This expresses their Christian faith. In some services the bishop sprinkles the congregation with holy water, as a reminder of their own baptism.

The Baptists, a Christian denomination, do not baptize babies. Babies are welcomed into the Church with a service of blessing, and members are only baptized when they are old enough to make a commitment for themselves. The baptism is an independent choice, as it is in a confirmation. The adult is fully immersed in water, symbolizing a spiritual cleansing and washing away of sins.

This jug contains chrism, a sacred oil. In some Roman Catholic confirmation services, the bishop makes the sign of the cross on the person's forehead with chrism.

Sacred text

Do you turn to Christ?

Do you repent of your sins?

Do you renounce evil?

Do you believe and trust in God the Father who made the world?

Do you believe and trust in his son, Jesus Christ, who redeemed mankind?

Do you believe and trust in the Holy Spirit who gives life to the people of God?

Questions asked during a confirmation service.

Being a Christian

*C*onfirmation confirms a person's faith. But what does it mean to be a member of the Christian Church? In some Christian denominations, you can only take Holy Communion if you have been confirmed. In others, you can take it before confirmation.

Holy Communion (also known as the Eucharist or Mass) usually takes place during a church service. A Christian eats a small piece of bread (symbolizing Christ's body) and sips some wine (symbolizing his blood). This reminds Christians of Christ's sacrifice when he was crucified.

Roman Catholic confirmations are often held on Pentecost Sunday, the day that celebrates the descent of the Holy Spirit. There is often a reception or small party after a confirmation service. This includes friends, family and the sponsor.

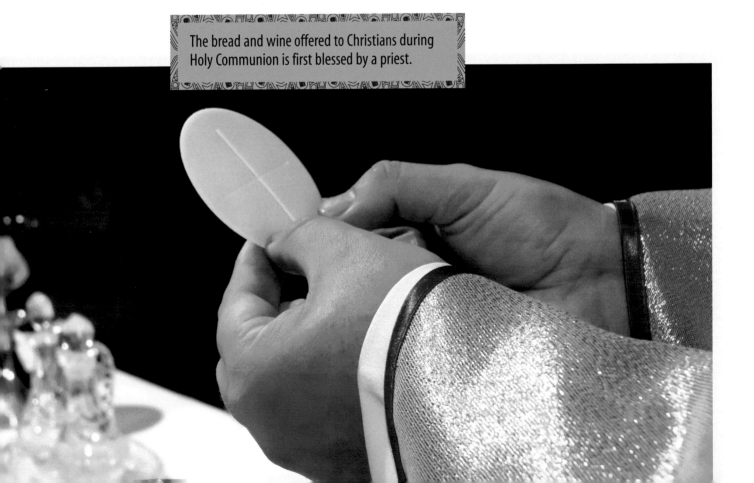

The bread and wine offered to Christians during Holy Communion is first blessed by a priest.

Newly confirmed young people are often given a gift, such as a Bible.

When a person receives the Holy Spirit, Christians believe that he or she receives seven gifts that will help them in their Christian life.

These gifts received by a Christian during confirmation are:

- wisdom
- understanding
- knowledge
- right judgement
- courage
- reverence
- awe and wonder

The newly-confirmed Christian is expected to show their commitment to their faith by attending church services regularly. Confirmed Christians should also behave in accordance with the Christian values and morals set out in the Bible. After confirmation, a Christian can sponsor someone else and be a guide in their faith and their coming of age rite.

FOCUS ON:
Quinceanera

The *quinceanera* is a South American coming of age ceremony for girls at the age of fifteen. It begins with a Roman Catholic Mass, a service at which there is a special blessing. It is followed by a large and often grand party for the girl celebrating her fifteenth birthday, her family and godparents. She often wears a new ball gown and lots of jewellery. The girl has the first dance (a waltz) with her father, to symbolize that he recognizes she is now a woman. The quinceanera traces its roots back to the Aztecs in South America over 2,500 years ago. Fifteen was the age at which most girls celebrated their coming of age and became women in Aztec society.

Preparing to come of age

*M*ost Jewish children take part in a coming of age ceremony. It is a time when a young person is publicly recognized as an active member of the Jewish community. The coming of age ceremony for a Jewish boy takes place on his 13th birthday, and for a Jewish girl on her 12th birthday. A Jewish boy becomes an adult according to Jewish law on his 13th birthday. A Jewish girl becomes an adult according to Jewish law on her 12th birthday.

When a Jewish boy reaches adulthood he is called *bar mitzvah* (son of the commandment). A girl is called *bat mitzvah* (daughter of the commandment). These names are also given to the ceremonies that celebrate a boy or girl's coming of age.

In Judaism, boys and girls are considered spiritually mature at the ages of 13 and 12 respectively. At this age, they enter the covenant with God. The covenant is the relationship or agreement between a Jew and God, that God will never leave the Jewish people and a Jewish person will follow God's commandments. There are 613 rules or commandments to follow. These are laid down in the Torah, the sacred collection of Jewish teachings. These 613 rules are called *mitzvot*, the plural of mitzvah.

In preparation for their bar or bat mitzvah, children may also prepare some thoughts of their own on a section of the Torah.

The bat or bar mitzvah ceremony is a popular way to mark a Jewish child's coming of age. It symbolizes that the individual is now a responsible member of the Jewish community. However, at 13 or 12 years old any child born to a Jewish mother automatically becomes a full member of the Jewish faith, whether or not this coming of age is celebrated. Months before the bat or bar mitzvah, the child prepares for the ceremony. They must learn off by heart a section from the Torah and some prayers.

For several years, children prepare by going to Hebrew or religious school. Here they learn the Hebrew language and Jewish history, belief, customs and culture. There is much to prepare before a bat or bar mitzvah celebration. If the party after the ceremony is a grand one, parents may spend a long time preparing for it (see page 16).

MODERN DEBATE:
GIRLS

Different branches of Judaism have varying views about the role of girls and women in their faith. Very strict Orthodox Jews believe that the Torah must be followed word for word. They do not publically mark a girl's coming of age. Instead, they have a small celebratory meal at home. However, a boy's coming of age is marked with a public ceremony, the bar mitzvah.

Liberal Jews believe that Judaism should adapt to modern times, and give girls a similar coming of age ceremony to boys. Liberal Jews mark a girl's coming of age with a bat mitzvah ceremony.

Do you think the Torah should be followed strictly, so that only a boy's coming of age is celebrated? Or should both boys and girls celebrate their coming of age?

Many children hope to have their bar or bat mitzvah by the Western Wall in Jerusalem. The Western Wall is one of the most holy Jewish sites.

Bar and bat mitzvah

The bar or bat mitzvah ceremony usually takes place in a synagogue on the Sabbath following the boy's 13th birthday. A rabbi, a Jewish spiritual leader, leads the service. The synagogue is usually packed with family and friends. The occasion is a chance for members of the Jewish community to come together to celebrate their religion and the passing on of tradition and values as a child grows into adulthood.

On the day of the ceremony (usually a Friday or Saturday), the boy or girl receives a *tallit*. This is a prayer shawl worn for morning prayers. It is a white rectangular piece of material with a fringe of 613 knots or tassels, to remind the wearer of God's commandments (see page 12).

In Orthodox synagogues, a boy is given a *tefillin*. This consists of two black leather boxes with straps. They contain the *shema* prayer, which tells Jews to love God with all their head and heart. One tefillin is placed on the head; the other is tied on the left arm so that it rests against the heart, and the straps are wrapped around the arms. The boy, now considered a young man, must wear the tefillin at morning prayers each day, except for the Sabbath and festivals.

Jewish boys are shown how to put on their tefillin in preparation for their bar mitzvah.

At the bar or bat mitzvah the child is invited, for the first time, to read in Hebrew from the Torah, or to read the blessing on the Torah reading. This public reading celebrates the transition from child to adult. Only adults (men only in Orthodox Judaism) are allowed to read from the Torah in the synagogue. The readings from the Torah are arranged so that the whole of the Torah is read during a year. The child reads from the point at which the previous reading stopped.

The father then gives his blessing and thanks God for having brought the child to maturity. He declares that, in terms of Judaism, the boy or girl is now responsible for his or her actions, and he rejoices that his child is now an adult. The service ends with the rabbi reciting the *kiddush*, a special prayer said over a cup of wine to mark the Sabbath or a Jewish holy day.

Sacred text

And you must commit yourselves wholeheartedly to these commands I am giving you today.

Repeat them again and again to your children. Talk about them when you are at home and when you are away on a journey, when you are lying down and when you are getting up again.

Tie them to your hands as a reminder, and wear them on your forehead.

Write them on the doorposts of your house and on your gates.

Deuteronomy, 6:6–9

The origins of wearing the tefillin are expressed in this part of the Shema prayer.

15

Becoming a Jewish adult

The bar or bat mitzvah is an opportunity for Jewish families to come together. After the ceremony, the parents arrange a meal (seudah) for the young person's relatives and friends. At this occasion the young adult delivers a sermon of thanks. Sometimes guests bring gifts, such as a Jewish prayer book (siddur), a tallit or tefillin. A large, elaborate party with music and dancing often follows. Many Orthodox Jews disapprove of this type of celebration.

The bar mitzvah boy takes on the full religious responsibilities of a Jewish adult. He is allowed to wear the ritual clothes (the tallit and tefillin). He can be counted as one of the ten men (the minyan) in the synagogue. Ten men must be present for a service to take place. The adult can also read from the Torah in the synagogue.

Whether or not a boy has taken part in a ceremony to mark his transition to adulthood, boys over 13 are allowed to sign contracts and to testify (give evidence) in religious courts. According to Jewish religious law a boy can marry at 13, and a girl at 12. However, the Talmud (the collection of writings on Jewish law) recommends ages 18 to 24. Marriage at 13 is not legal in many countries.

After the bar or bat mitzvah, family and friends often celebrate with a party.

FOCUS ON:
The Torah

The Torah is written in Hebrew, which is a language without vowels (the letters a, e, i, o, u). It takes a lot of skill to follow the words that are handwritten on the scroll. When the scroll is unwound it is over 60 metres long. It is unwound to the correct place and placed on the *bimah*, or reading desk. A *yad* or pointer is used to follow the words as the person reads, because the surface of the scroll must not be touched. Men (and women in Liberal Jewish synagogues) take turns to read from the Torah. This is considered a great honour.

The learning that starts in preparation for the bar or bat mitzvah ceremony is expected to continue long after the day. The Jewish adult will continue to develop his or her faith and belief. He or she is expected to keep the 613 Jewish mitzvot. These include: honour your parents; offer hospitality; help the poor and needy; visit the sick; be friendly and peaceful; defend the Jewish faith.

At each end of the Torah is a wooden roller, around which the scroll is wound.

Preparing for adulthood

There is no single ceremony to mark the transition from child to adult in Islam. Instead, Muslims (followers of the Islamic religion) are expected to bring up children with Islamic values, honouring the Islamic way of life.

From an early age, children learn about Islam. When they reach the age of four, they start to learn parts of the Qur'an in Arabic. The Qur'an is the Islamic holy book. In Pakistan and some other parts of the world, a ceremony called *bismillah* celebrates this first stage in a child's learning. Bismillah is the first word in the Qur'an, and means 'in the name of God'.

At a bismillah ceremony, the four year-old sits in front of the Qur'an, dressed in smart clothes. He or she recites the *Sura al-Fatihah* (the opening verses of the Qur'an) and sometimes writes out the letters of the Arabic alphabet. The guests pray for the child's knowledge. Then they all share sweet foods. The bismillah ceremony marks the beginning of a child's religious education. From now on, the child attends the *madrasah*, a school at the mosque, the Muslim place of worship. Here the child begins to learn more of the Qur'an off by heart.

Puberty often marks the time when a young person takes on more responsibility as a Muslim. Boys who have reached puberty are expected to attend the mosque for public prayers and to fast during *Ramadan* (see page 23).

Children often memorize the shorter chapters at the end of the Qur'an, before they move on to the longer chapters at the start.

This young Muslim girl is wearing a hijab. The word hijab means 'barrier' or 'screen' in Arabic.

MODERN DEBATE:
THE HIJAB

Today Muslims live all over the world, in countries that do not follow modern Islamic law and where another religion may be dominant. Muslim laws and practices for young people are sometimes at odds with the customs and behaviour of other young people in the country. For instance, in countries such as France, some schools do not allow girls to wear the hijab. Yet, wearing the hijab is extremely important to some Muslim girls.

While some Muslim girls may be told to wear the hijab by their parents, others want and choose to wear it themselves. Muslim teaching is that a woman's standard of behaviour and dress should come from her own desire to please Allah. Yet, in Saudi Arabia, where Islam is the official religion, girls and women must wear the hijab by law.

Should Muslim girls be allowed to choose for themselves whether to wear the hijab, regardless of their family or where they live?

In many Muslim communities, when a girl has her first period, she begins to wear the *hijab* or veil. Wearing a veil is a personal statement that can have different meanings for different individuals. For many women, wearing a veil is about dressing modestly, as Muslim men are also expected to do. It is a statement of their faith.

Sacred text

In the Name of Allah, Most Gracious, Most Merciful. Praise be to Allah, the Cherisher and Sustainer of the Worlds. Most Gracious, Most Merciful. Master of the Day of Judgement. You alone we worship, and Your aid alone we seek. Show us the straight way. The way of those on whom You have bestowed Your grace, those whose portion is not wrath and who go not astray.

Sura al-Fatihah

A spiritual education

Following the bismillah, a child's education continues as he or she attends school at the mosque. At a mosque school, Muslim children study the Qur'an and learn about the Islamic way of life. They read and recite the Qur'an in Arabic, even if this is not their first language.

In Malaysia, Islam is the official religion. Here some ten year-old boys and girls take part in a ceremony called *ameen*. This marks the time when a child has read the 114 *surahs* or chapters of the Qur'an. He or she must be able to correctly read out all the words, which are written in Arabic, before some invited guests, including the child's teacher. When the reading is complete, the child kisses the hands of his Qur'an teacher, his parents and each of the guests. The child then joins the guests to eat a feast of yellow rice and specially prepared foods. The ceremony and the meal celebrate the successful spiritual education of the child.

Although the ameen ceremony is for both boys and girls, for girls it is carried out only in front of women. No men are allowed. Girls often wear white during the ceremony, to symbolize purity.

These girls are helping each other learn to read the Qur'an in Arabic.

20

It is important for a Muslim to read and understand the Islamic holy book, the Qur'an.

According to the law in Iran, where Islam is the official religion, a girl becomes a woman on her ninth birthday. This means that she can marry at nine years old. However, many other countries (whether or not Islam is the official religion) do not allow a girl to marry at this age.

To mark a Muslim girl's coming of age, a ceremony called *takleaf* takes place. The young girl wears a white hijab which covers her body completely. The hijab is a piece of clothing that covers a Muslim woman from head to toe, with only her hands, face and feet still visible. By keeping her body hidden, the hijab is thought to protect a woman's modesty and keep her pure.

In Saudi Arabia, a Muslim girl chooses her first hijab when she has her first period. It is said that she enters the hijab shop as a girl to choose her hijab and comes out as a woman.

From the age of nine years, a Muslim girl is not allowed to play with boys, apart from her brothers. She must behave modestly and observe the same rules as grown women.

FOCUS ON:
The Qur'an

Muslims believe that the Qur'an contains the words of Allah (God). Muhammad (pbuh), Allah's prophet and messenger, learned the words off by heart when the angel Gabriel spoke to him. A devout Muslim also learns the Qur'an off by heart. This tradition ensures that the words of Allah remain unchanged. The Qur'an is the Muslim holy book. Muslims who learn the words of the Qur'an off by heart are given the title of *hafiz*.

21

Becoming a Muslim adult

Coming of age in Islam is marked by a continuous process of education. On reaching puberty, a young girl or boy is expected to take a more active part in the Muslim practices that then follow and honour the Islamic way of life. These are underpinned by the five pillars of Islam.

A Muslim adult must also follow *shari'ah* (or path), the code of behaviour and laws taken from the Qur'an and from the teachings of Muhammad (pbuh). This is a system of laws and customs governing Muslims' political, economic and social relations.

The five pillars of Islam

1. *Shahadah*: affirming faith daily

Every day a Muslim affirms his or her faith, repeating the shahadah which begins 'There is no God but Allah, and Muhammad (pbuh) is his messenger.' This is the basis of Islamic faith. A Muslim is expected to recite this statement out loud, with total sincerity, fully understanding what it means. Reciting the shahadah three times in front of witnesses is all that anyone need do to become a Muslim.

2. *Salat*: praying five times a day

Namaz, or daily prayers, are said every day at dawn, noon, mid-afternoon, sunset and night. Prayers are always said facing the holy city of Makkah (Mecca) in Saudi Arabia.

During prayer, Muslims lower themselves to the ground to show humbleness before Allah.

The pilgrimage to Makkah takes place between the sixth and 12th day of *Dhu al-Hijjah*, the twelfth month of the Islamic calendar.

3. *Zakah*: helping the poor and needy

Each Muslim is expected to give 2.5 percent of their income to support the poor.

4. *Sawm*: fasting during Ramadan

During the holy month of Ramadan, Muslims fast from sunrise to sunset. They believe that the Qur'an was revealed to Muhammad (pbuh) during the month of Ramadan, which lasts 29 or 30 days. Children, the elderly and the sick do not have to fast. A young person's first fast during Ramadan is a rite of passage into adulthood that shows their commitment to Islamic values. It helps them develop self-control, and shows that they have submitted to Allah.

5. *Hajj*: going an a pilgrimage

Every Muslim who is able and can afford to must make a pilgrimage or religious journey, called Hajj, to Makkah, the birthplace of Muhammad (pbuh).

Marking coming of age

*T*raditionally, it is a Hindu's duty (*dharma*) to observe the 16 *samskaras*, or rites of passage. However, today the main samskaras that Hindus observe are the rites of birth, coming of age, marriage and death. Across the world, different Hindu communities mark the samskaras in different ways.

Hindus believe that all living things are caught in a continuous cycle of birth and death. When the soul reaches purity and understands true wisdom it can join *Brahman*, the ultimate reality from which everything comes and returns. They believe that observing the samskaras correctly can help a person to move through this cycle and finally achieve release or *moksha*, and join Brahman.

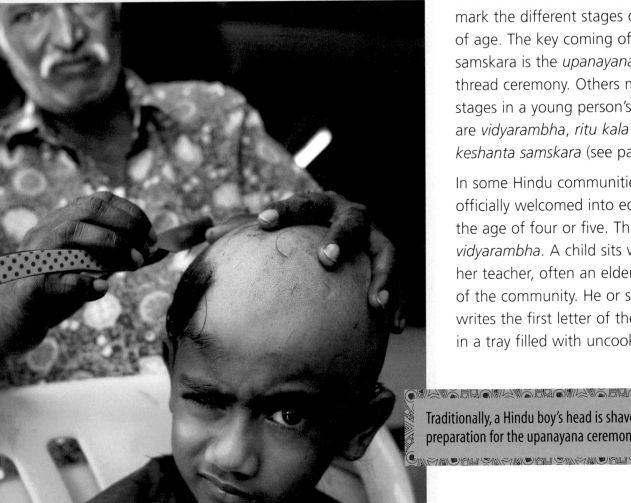

There are several samskaras that mark the different stages of coming of age. The key coming of age samskara is the *upanayana*, the sacred thread ceremony. Others mark different stages in a young person's life. These are *vidyarambha*, *ritu kala* and *keshanta samskara* (see page 29).

In some Hindu communities, a child is officially welcomed into education at the age of four or five. This is called *vidyarambha*. A child sits with his or her teacher, often an elderly member of the community. He or she then writes the first letter of the alphabet in a tray filled with uncooked rice.

Traditionally, a Hindu boy's head is shaved in preparation for the upanayana ceremony.

The Hindu holy books are the Vedas. Veda means knowledge.

The upanayana, or sacred thread ceremony, is a very important samskara. This is the main coming of age ceremony for a boy and takes place between the ages of seven and 12. This is when the boy begins his study of the Vedas, the sacred books of Hindus. The ceremony is held on a lucky day. Traditionally, an astrologer works out the date by studying the movements of the planets and stars. Sometimes, the vidyarambha and the upanayana are celebrated on the same day.

In India, only boys from the top three castes (social groups) – Brahmins, Kshatriyas and Vaishayas – take part in this ceremony (see page 29). In the past, girls did not take part in the upanayana, but today a few girls also take part. Before the ceremony, the young person learns about the meaning and significance of the ceremony.

FOCUS ON:
The Vedas

The Vedas are four collections of sacred writings, and the earliest Hindu sacred books. The words were passed down for hundreds of years by word of mouth, and were only written down in about 1400 CE. Each Veda contains mantras, verses written in the ancient language of Sanskrit.

25

The sacred thread ceremony

*U*panayana literally means 'getting closer to God'. Traditionally, the ceremony marked the beginning of a child's life as a student, at around eight years old. The child would devote himself to study, and would then leave his family to study with a guru.

Sacred text

O Divine mother, our hearts are filled with darkness. Please make this darkness distant from us and promote illumination within us.

Gayatri Mantra, The Rig Veda, 10:16:3

Today the ceremony usually takes place between the ages of seven and 12. A Hindu priest chooses the date and time of the sacred thread ceremony, to make sure that it will be lucky for the boy. Although the child often stays with his family – only a few girls take part – the ceremony marks the beginning of his spiritual education and his spiritual birth. On the day of the ceremony, the child bathes and puts on new clothes. Sometimes his head is shaved. The ceremony takes place at home or in a temple where sweet-smelling incense is burned.

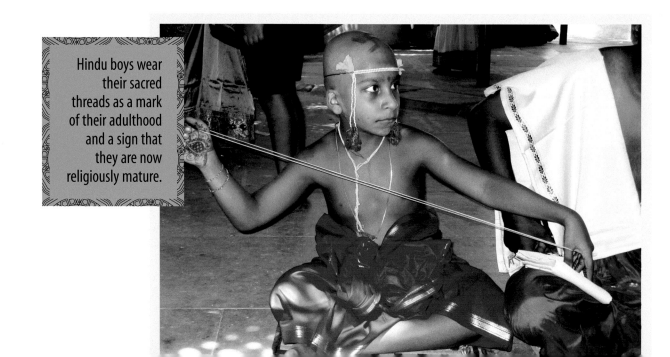

Hindu boys wear their sacred threads as a mark of their adulthood and a sign that they are now religiously mature.

A Hindu priest ties a loop of cotton thread, usually around the child's left shoulder to the right side of his waist. The thread is made of three strands of cotton. Often it is sprinkled with holy water from the River Ganges to make it sacred. The sacred thread symbolizes religious maturity and adulthood. The priest then says, 'May this sacred thread destroy my ignorance, bring me long life and increase my understanding'. The boy repeats this.

The priest, who now becomes the child's guru, teaches him the gayatri mantra and gives him a spiritual name to signify his 'second birth'. The priest tells him to repeat the gayatri mantra every day in prayer. Flowers and grains of rice are offered to God as part of worship, too.

After the ceremony, the child wraps the thread around the thumb of his right hand. The thread shows that he is 'twice-born'. The child promises to study the Vedas and to serve his teachers. Everyone shares some *prasad*, food which has been blessed. The ceremony closes as the child offers gifts to his guru.

FOCUS ON:
The threads

There are several beliefs about what the three threads stand for. They symbolize different things to different communities of Hindus. Some believe they represent the three Hindu gods Brahma (creator), Vishnu (protector) and Shiva (destroyer). These gods (like the many other Hindu gods) are aspects of Brahman, the invisible ultimate reality or great power. Others believe that the threads represent pure mind, word and action. For some Hindus, the threads act as a reminder of their obligation to teachers, parents and God. The knot in the middle represents the formless Brahman, the pure form of energy at the centre of everything.

Becoming a Hindu adult

Hindus believe that a person has two births: their physical birth from their mother and a spiritual birth and identity which occurs at the upanayana ceremony. The child symbolically accepts a spiritual teacher as father and the Vedas as mother.

When a man marries, three more threads are added to the sacred thread. This reflects the increase in his responsibilities. Some people add a thread for each child they have. The thread is never taken off, but when it wears out it is replaced by a new thread in a special ceremony.

Hindus are expected to read the Vedas carefully throughout their lives. After his upanayana ceremony, a Hindu boy can begin to study the Vedas.

Other less significant samskaras relating to coming of age include the *keshanta samskara* and *ritu kala*. As a boy reaches puberty, hair begins to grow on his face. In some Hindu communities when the boy first shaves it means he has come of age. A ceremony to celebrate this takes place either in the temple or at home. This is called keshanta samskara. When a young girl starts her periods, the ritu kala ceremony marks the event. She is given a sari and jewellery.

A Hindu adult can observe four *yogas* or paths during his or her spiritual journey. These are knowledge, meditation, devotion and acting selflessly or good works. Following these paths helps to release a Hindu from the cycle of birth and rebirth. This freedom from rebirth is called moksha.

MODERN DEBATE:

THE CASTE SYSTEM

Traditionally, an Indian – India is a mostly Hindu country – is born into a particular caste, or social group. Lower caste Indians may not be allowed to marry someone from a higher caste and they may not be allowed to perform better paid jobs. The lower group of castes, the so-called untouchables, were also once forced to live outside villages.

Some Indians still believe that the caste system should stay in place and that it provides order and structure to Indian society. Other Indians believe that the caste system discriminates against lower caste people and should be ended.

Do you think the caste system is right or wrong?

The ritu kala ceremony marks the end of childhood for a Hindu girl and her joining of the Hindu adult community. The ceremony also celebrates a girl's coming of age both spiritually and physically.

Preparing to come of age

There are two ceremonies that mark important developments in the life of a Sikh child and adult. The first of these is the *dastaar bandi*, a ceremony that takes place when a Sikh boy comes of age. The second is the *amrit*, which takes place when a boy becomes an adult and joins the Sikh community.

In the Sikh religion there are five key signs of faith and commitment. They are known as the five K's (see page 34). One of these is not to cut one's hair. To keep the hair tidy, symbolizing the order in a Sikh's life, the hair is kept in a *dastaar* (turban). Young boys tie their hair in a bun and cover it with a piece of white cloth. Girls usually wear their hair long in plaits or tied up in a bun. Between the ages of 14 and 16, young Sikhs practise tying and wearing the turban. The material is over five metres long and a metre wide, so it can feel quite heavy. It takes a while to get used to wearing it.

Young people aged between 14 and 16 tie their first turban in a coming of age rite called dastaar bandi. The young person sits in front of the Guru Granth Sahib, the Sikh holy book. An older relation ties the turban. The granthi (the person who looks after the Guru Granth Sahib) explains why the boy must keep his hair long and wear a turban. Prayers are recited.

A Sikh boy's long hair is wound into a bun, called a *rishi* knot, and secured on top of his head. The length of material that makes up a turban is then wound around the bun and the boy's head to create his turban.

The spiritual Sikh coming of age rite is open to anyone who wants to commit to the Sikh religion and join the *khalsa*, the community of Sikhs. This sacred ceremony is called amrit. People taking part in amrit do so of their own choice, but they must be mature enough to take on the responsibilities of being a member of the Sikh faith. Men and women of any age can take part in the amrit ceremony. Most Sikhs prefer to take amrit on *Vaisakhi*, the anniversary of the day when Guru Gobind Singh introduced the rite, in 1699 CE.

A Sikh ceremonially drinks the sacred amrit as he is welcomed into the khalsa.

FOCUS ON:
Khalsa

The amrit ceremony was first introduced in 1699 by Guru Gobind Singh, when he founded the khalsa, a community of Sikhs who would honour Sikh values. At this time, Muslim rulers in the Punjab were persecuting Sikhs. At a gathering of Sikhs, the Guru called for them to come forward to form a group to defend their religion. One man stepped forward. He went into a tent with the Guru. The Guru came out holding a bloody sword. Four other men stepped forward, each prepared to die for his belief. Each time he disappeared into the tent and only the Guru came out, his sword stained with blood. The crowd thought the men had been killed. Then the five Sikhs appeared, dressed in saffron-coloured robes. The crowd was amazed at their bravery. These men were the first five to belong to the khalsa, the pure ones. They are called the *panj piare* – the beloved ones.

The amrit ceremony

To prepare for amrit, an individual washes his or her hair, puts on the turban and clean clothes, and wears the five K's (see page 34). The ceremony must be held in front of the Guru Granth Sahib. Any place where the Sikh holy book is kept becomes a gurdwara, the Sikh place of worship. Only Sikhs who have already taken amrit can be present at the initiation ceremony.

Five Sikhs who have already taken amrit and who represent the panj piare carry out the ceremony. A sixth reads from the Guru Granth Sahib. They begin by repeating the duties of members of the khalsa. They explain the code of conduct of its members, and ask if the person taking amrit agrees to follow it. If he or she agrees, they read from the Guru Granth Sahib.

The preparation of the amrit now begins. This is the name of the drink that is prepared in ceremonial way. It is a mixture of sugar and water, prepared in a steel bowl. The five Sikhs conducting the ceremony stir it with a double-handed sword called a *khanda*. They also recite five special prayers called *banis*. Then those present recite the *ardas*, the prayer said by Sikhs after any ceremony and in the morning and evening.

These five Sikhs are preparing the amrit drink before the ceremony. Each Sikh is holding a double-handed sword which they use to stir the drink.

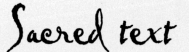

This girl is taking part in the amrit ceremony. Her face is being sprinkled with amrit by one of the five Sikhs leading the ceremony.

Kneeling in the 'warrior' position, with the left knee raised and the right knee touching the ground, the person taking amrit cups his or her right hand over their left hand. The Sikh leading the ceremony sprinkles amrit into the cup of their hand. They drink the amrit five times, repeating: 'Waheguru Ji Ka Khalsa, Waheguru Ji Ki Fateh' (The Pure Belong to God, Victory to God). Amrit is sprinkled five times on his or her hair and eyes. Any amrit that is left over is drunk from the bowl by the others present. Everyone present recites the *Mool Mantar*, a prayer that expresses the basic beliefs of Sikhism. There are readings from the Guru Granth Sahib and an explanation of the rules of Sikhism. Then the ardas prayer is repeated.

The ceremony ends with the eating of the *karah parshad*, a sacred pudding that has been blessed. It is made from semolina, sugar and *ghee* (liquid butter). Those taking part in the ceremony eat it from a shared bowl, symbolizing the community of the khalsa.

Sikhs believe that taking amrit ensures they will have everlasting life, after their physical death, if they continue to obey the teachings of Sikhism.

Sacred text

There is One God
Whose Name is True
The Creator
Without fear
Without hate
Immortal
Beyond the cycle of
    birth and death
Self-revealing
As Grace.

The Mool Mantar

Becoming a Sikh adult

*E*very Sikh who has taken amrit is required to be an active member of the Sikh community. As well as wearing the five K's, he or she is expected not to: smoke or take drugs; eat halal or kosher meat (an animal that has been killed by ritual slaughter, according to Muslim or Jewish rites); commit adultery (have sex with someone who is not their husband or wife); or cut their hair. If a Sikh breaks these vows, he or she has to take amrit again, after a suitable time.

After becoming a member of the khalsa, men adopt the name of Singh (lion) and women take the name Kaur (princess) as part of their names. The fact that everyone takes the same name symbolizes that Sikhs are all members of one family.

To mark their membership of the khalsa, Sikhs agree to wear the five K's. These are:

- *kesh* or uncut hair, wrapped up in a turban

- the *kangha*, a small comb used to keep the long hair tidy, a symbol of order in life

- the *kara*, a stainless steel bracelet whose circle stands for God who has no beginning or end

- the *kachera*, white shorts worn under clothes, to symbolize purity and modesty

- the *kirpan*, a symbolic short sword that reminds Sikhs always to fight for the truth and defend the weak.

These young Sikh women are praying. Sikhs are expected to pray regularly to focus their minds on God.

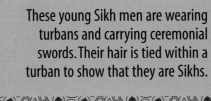

These young Sikh men are wearing turbans and carrying ceremonial swords. Their hair is tied within a turban to show that they are Sikhs.

MODERN DEBATE:
WEARING THE TURBAN

In some countries, such as France, the law does not allow children to wear any religious clothing at school. France is a secular country and wants to keep the state and religion separate. For this reason, the French believe that all children should wear the same clothes to school.

For Sikhs, wearing a turban is a statement of identity. The wearing of a turban is key to the Sikh faith and a fundamental part of their religion. Sikh boys have been expelled from French schools for wearing their turbans. An organization called the United Sikhs is currently taking the boys' case to the Court of Human Rights.

Do you think Sikhs should be allowed to wear turbans to school, or should all school children wear the same uniform?

FOCUS ON:
Guru Granth Sahib

Sikhs believe there were ten Gurus, or teachers, each chosen in succession. The tenth Guru chose not to appoint a new human Guru, as the previous Gurus had done. Instead, he said that in future the Sikhs' guide on their spiritual journey would be their holy book, the Guru Granth Sahib. This was compiled by Guru Arjan and placed in the most sacred Sikh shrine, the Golden Temple in Amritsar, India, in 1604. It contains hymns written by Guru Nanak and other Gurus. It is unique among holy books because it also contains hymns written by Hindu and Muslim holy men. The book contains 1430 pages and 3384 hymns. Every copy is printed so that the hymns are always on the same page.

Members of the khalsa (and many other Sikhs) know by heart the five sacred prayers, which they recite each day as a way of meditating upon God's name. Sikhs believe there is a part of God inside each person. This belief encourages them to serve the community, Sikhs and non-Sikhs alike. The idea of *sewa* or service is central to Sikhism. It may take the form of giving money to help others, or cooking and cleaning in the gurdwara.

35

Coming of age

$\mathcal{B}$uddhism spread from India to other Southeast Asian countries such as Thailand, Sri Lanka and Japan. There are many Buddhist traditions, based largely on its geographical spread. Some branches of Buddhism have ceremonies for ordination, when a person becomes a monk or nun. Others have ceremonies for ordinary followers to mark their commitment to Buddhism. There is no one single rite of passage.

Zen is a school of Buddhism, very popular in Japan, which emphasizes the practice of meditation – deep attention or awareness – as a means to find awakening. In some Zen Buddhist practices, *jukai* is a ceremony to mark an adult's coming of age and their choice to commit to the Buddhist way of life. There can be variations on the ceremony for younger people.

Before jukai, a person will have been practising as a Buddhist. This means regular meditation, and attending classes at a Buddhist centre or temple led by a monk or nun. Jukai takes place in a Buddhist centre or temple. Accompanied by chanting, the person takes The Three Refuges (see page 38). Reciting these symbolizes their commitment to the three elements of Buddhism: the *sangha* (a monastery or strong community of Buddhists), the Buddha, and *dharma* (the path or way of Buddhism).

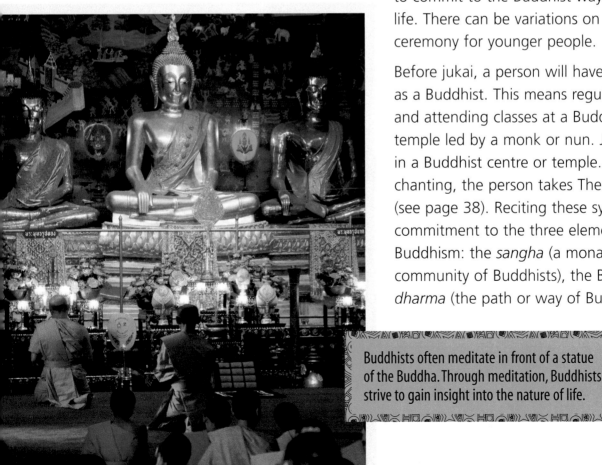

Buddhists often meditate in front of a statue of the Buddha. Through meditation, Buddhists strive to gain insight into the nature of life.

Before the ceremony, the person sews a *rakusu*. This is a piece of material worn around the neck. It is made from patches of cloth sewn together and it symbolizes the Buddha's own robe. He made this from scraps of material found in the streets, which he dyed saffron yellow and sewed together. The person taking jukai gives the monk or nun the rakusu. During the ceremony, the rakusu is given back to the individual. In some traditions, a new Buddhist name is written on the back of the material. The name is usually in the language of the particular school. A person in a Zen jukai ceremony will receive a Japanese name. In the Tibetan tradition, the name will be in Tibetan.

Sacred text

To the Buddha,
  I go for refuge.
To the dharma,
  I go for refuge.
To the sangha,
  I go for refuge.

The Three Refuges

The person makes a public acceptance of the five Buddhist precepts or principles by reciting them. They are: to avoid harming living things; to avoid taking things that have not been freely given; to live a wholesome life; to avoid speaking unkindly or lying; to avoid alcohol and drugs. These precepts are not commandments or rules. They are principles by which a Buddhist is expected to live. The Three Refuges and The Five Precepts are the basic moral code for any Buddhist who is not a member of the sangha (a monk or nun). After receiving jukai, the person wears the rakusu or a *wagessa* (a strip of cloth tied with a decorative knot).

Spiritual education

In many parts of Southeast Asia, puberty is a time when a child may decide to enter a Buddhist monastery, or sangha. In Theravadan schools of Buddhism in Myanmar (Burma), young boys enter a Buddhist monastery for a short time to become a novice, or trainee monk. The ceremony to mark this is called *shinbyu*. It is considered an important stage in the boy's life and spiritual education. The training is open to boys as young as five, but most attend before the age of 19.

The child is dressed in fine clothes and rides on a horse. Ahead of him, a man carries a robe to offer to the Buddha. Behind him, friends and family carry gifts, such as books on Buddhist teachings, umbrellas, mats, pillows and palm-leaf fans. Local musicians provide the music.

The boy's head is shaved. He changes from his ordinary clothes into a monk's saffron-yellow robes. He takes with him an alms bowl, into which he will receive food. He takes The Three Refuges (see page 36) and then the precepts. A senior monk becomes his teacher and gives him a Buddhist name.

Before a boy can enter a Buddhist monastery, his head must be shaved. This marks that he has given up all worldly, or material, things.

The senior monk or abbot talks about the Buddhist teachings. Then the young boy enters the monastery and stays with the monks for up to a month. He can leave the monastery and return home at any time. Some boys decide to stay on in the monastery and become monks when they are 20 years old.

Girls can also become nuns and spend a period of time in a monastery, but there is no special ceremony for this. Some girls in Myanmar also take part in a non-religious ceremony to mark their coming of age, in which their ears are pierced.

FOCUS ON:
The Buddha

The shinbyu ceremony symbolizes the entry of Prince Rahula, the son of Siddhattha Gotama (the Buddha) into Buddhism. Siddhattha Gotama was an Indian nobleman who founded Buddhism in the 6th century. He left his riches and wealth behind him, in a physical and spiritual journey to find the causes of the suffering he saw in the world and a way to end it. He attained enlightenment, an understanding of the truth of how things are. Those who followed Gotama's teachings called him the Buddha, meaning 'the one who knows'.

Some boys stay in the monastery until they reach adulthood and become monks. Girls may also stay within the monastery, and become nuns.

Apache and humanist rituals

ifferent cultures around the world have their own customs to mark a young person's coming of age. In Arizona and New Mexico, members of the Apache peoples celebrate the sunrise ceremony, or *na'ii'ees*. This is a four-day rite held shortly after the start of a girl's first period. Preparations for the ceremony take months. The girl must build up her strength to endure the rite which is very challenging, both emotionally and physically. Getting through it helps to boost the girl's self esteem.

Over the course of four days, friends and family come together. A godmother, a medicine man and a friend who has already experienced the rite guide the girl, encouraging her when she loses energy and commitment.

First her face is painted white, with a mixture of pollen and clay. She wears a piece of abalone shell on her forehead. For four days, she takes part in sacred dances, singing and rituals. She is taught about what it means to be a woman, and the story of the White Painted Woman (see box on p41) is acted out. This helps the girl to connect to the spirits of the past.

In the early 1900s, the US government forbade Apaches from gathering together. The sunrise ceremony was carried out in secret, but in 1978 the law changed to allow the ceremony to take place again.

Young Apache women are covered in pollen and clay to represent the White Painted Woman.

In England in the 19th century, young upper-class women were 'introduced' into society when they came of age. Balls were held for them, at which they mixed with other upper-class young people and looked for a suitable husband.

Humanists have no attachment to religious beliefs; they do not believe in a god, gods or spirits. To mark a person's transition to adulthood they may hold a ceremony which is sometimes called a civic confirmation. This is especially popular in some Scandinavian countries, where groups of young people gather together on camps or courses. Here they reflect on the responsibilities that adulthood brings, and celebrate their journey from child to adult.

For some people, their coming of age is marked simply by a party. This often has no religious significance. The party is held when they reach the age at which they are considered to be an adult. This may be age 18 or 21, depending on their country.

FOCUS ON:
The White Painted Woman

In Apache belief, the White Painted Woman was the first woman. She survived the Flood in an abalone shell. The Sun and Rain gave her two sons. After killing a giant that was attacking the Apache people, the sons returned to their mother. She greeted their return with delight, and established a puberty rite for all Apache girls. As the White Painted Woman grew old she walked eastwards, towards the Sun. Here, she met her younger self, and merged with it. She has been born again in each generation.

Japanese and African rituals

Every year in Japan, on the second Monday in January, there is a national holiday to mark Coming of Age Day. This is called Seijin Shiki. Young men and women who will reach their 20th birthday in that year take part in the ceremony, which welcomes them into adulthood. In Japan, a person can legally vote in elections and drink alcohol at the age of 20. He or she also becomes responsible for their actions.

Across Japan, local government offices, large employers or schools organize the event. Local officials and invited speakers make speeches. The new adults pledge to be responsible members of society, and are sometimes presented with small gifts to mark the occasion.

Young women wear a brightly-coloured kimono called a *furisode*. The furisode is very expensive, so many women hire them for the day. Men wear dark suits or kimonos. The ceremony takes place in the morning, and after it many of the adults go on to celebrate at a party.

Seijin Shiki has its roots in an eighth-century rite called genpuku, which marked the transition to adulthood of male samurai warriors. Between the ages of 12 and 15, boys took on an adult name, changed their hairstyle and were treated as an adult.

The long, hanging sleeves of the furisode show that the woman who wears it is unmarried. Older married women wear kimonos with shorter sleeves.

These young Masai warriors perform the warrior 'jumping' dance when they reach adulthood. The higher they jump, the higher their warrior status will be.

In Africa, tribal coming of age rites are intended to build character and make the child aware of the demands of adulthood. There are usually separate rites for boys and girls. They provide them with the skills and confidence they will need in their adult lives.

The young person is first separated from their family and friends. This can be for just a day or for several months, depending on local practice. In some cases, the person is physically marked. This may be with circumcision or body decoration. During their time away from the community, the young person often makes and uses artworks to learn about the functions and beauty of objects. When they return to the community, the young person is an adult. There is a big celebration with music, dancing and feasting.

MODERN DEBATE:
CIRCUMCISION

In some African communities, such as the Xhosa tribe in South Africa, boys and girls are circumcised. This means that the foreskin of a boy's penis is cut off and the sexual organs of a girl are cut. Many traditional people within African communities wish to continue circumcising boys and girls – they argue the practice is part of their cultural history.

Other people believe circumcision is unhygenic and can cause infected wounds, pain and severe medical problems. Many people worldwide believe that circumcision, particularly of girls, is wrong. In some parts of Kenya, women are replacing circumcision with 'circumcision by words'. This is a coming of age week, when the girl spends time with other women and learns about issues of adult life such as reproduction, hygiene and dealing with peer pressure.

Do you think circumcision is right or wrong?

43

Religion and coming of age: a summary

Religion	Preparation	Coming of age ceremony	Venue
Christianity	Confirmation classes, studying the Bible and discussing what it means to be a Christian.	Confirmation service – for both boys and girls. Ages vary according to denomination. Led by priest or bishop.	Usually in a church or cathedral, but sometimes in a school.
Judaism	Classes to learn Hebrew and to learn about Jewish history, culture and religion.	Bar mitzvah for boys at 13. Bat mitzvah (some branches of Judaism) for girls at 12.	In a synagogue.
Islam	Learning Arabic and developing an understanding and awareness of Islamic beliefs and practices.	Generally no particular ceremony but a young person is expected to continue to be more active in observing Islamic practices and principles.	No particular ceremony or venue.
Hinduism	Study of the Vedas – mostly for boys, aged between seven and 12.	Sacred thread given to the young person to symbolize religious maturity and adulthood.	At home or in a Hindu temple.
Sikhism	Making an independent decision to become a full member of the Sikh religion.	Ceremony in front of the Guru Granth Sahib, led by six Sikhs who have already taken amrit. Ritual preparation of amrit and drinking of amrit. Special prayers.	In a gurdwara.
Buddhism	No particular preparation apart from honouring Buddhist philosophy and practices.	In Zen Buddhism, the jukai led by a Buddhist monk or nun. In Myanmar Buddhism, the Shinbyu ceremony.	Jukai: in a Buddhist centre or temple. Shinbyu: in a Buddhist monastery.

Gifts	Celebrations	Responsibilities after coming of age
Usually a Bible.	Reception or small gathering afterwards.	Confirmed Christian can become a sponsor for other people being confirmed. Expected to attend church. Expected to honour Christian values.
The Torah, a tallit or tefillin.	Meal to celebrate often followed by a large party.	Boy can be counted as one of ten needed to be present in synagogue for reading of the Torah. Young person can read from the Torah in the synagogue. Young person is expected to honour the 613 mitzvot.
No particular ceremony or gifts.	No particular celebration.	Honour five pillars of Islam. Girls wear hijab.
Boy offers gifts to guru following the sacred thread ceremony. Girls given new clothes, sari and jewellery for ritu kala ceremony.	Sharing food that has been blessed.	Continuing study of the Vedas. To pursue paths of knowledge, meditation, devotion and acting selflessly.
No particular ceremony or gifts.	No particular celebration.	Sikhs agree to wear the five K's. Praying daily and honouring Sikh values.
No particular ceremony or gifts.	No particular celebration.	Honouring the Five Buddhist precepts. Living by Buddhist principles.

Glossary

adolescence time of change between childhood and adulthood

astrologer person who studies the stars and planets to determine their influence on human lives

baptism Christian ceremony in which parents and godparents vow to bring a child up in a Christian way

bishop senior priest in the Christian Church

catechism set of questions and answers summarizing the Christian faith

circumcision ritual procedure where the foreskin is cut off a boy's penis

confirmation coming of age rite in Christianity

denomination branch of a religion that shares core beliefs but has some different interpretations or ways of worshipping

Eastern Orthodox the national churches of Greece, Russia, and some Slavic states, which grew out of a split between the two main centres of Christianity in the 11th century: Rome and Constantinople.

enlightenment in Buddhism a state of 'awakening', or understanding the true nature of the universe, which leads to freedom from the cycle of birth, suffering, death and rebirth

ghee liquid part of butter that has been melted and chilled, so the liquid can be separated out

Guru teacher. In Sikhism, the title is used only for the first ten Sikh leaders and the Guru Granth Sahib.

Holy Communion sacrament observed in most Christian churches, in which bread and wine are taken as reminders of the last meal of Jesus Christ, and of his death

kimono traditional dress worn by Japanese women

mantra short, sacred Hindu text or prayer that is chanted or recited in repetition

mosque Muslim place of worship

Orthodox Judaism Judaism in which the laws of the Torah are strictly followed

priest person who leads the service in a Christian church

Protestant branch of Christianity that is separate from Roman Catholicism and Eastern Orthodoxy. Protestant churches do not recognize a central religious authority such as the Pope or the Patriarch, but see the Bible as the ultimate authority on Christian teaching.

rabbi Jewish spiritual leader

rite of passage ceremony to mark an important stage in a person's life, such as birth, marriage or death

ritual ceremony following a series of actions

Roman Catholic branch of Christianity that recognizes the Pope, also known as the Bishop of Rome, as its religious authority

Sabbath Jewish religious day of rest and worship.

sacrament an experience when a Christian believes he or she is receiving special blessings from God

sacred holy or worthy of religious respect and worship

Find out more

Books

Facts about Religions: The Facts about Hinduism. Alison Cooper, (Hodder Wayland, 2004)

Religious Signs and Symbols: Judaism/Christianity/Hinduism/Islam. Cath Senker, (Wayland, 2008)

Sacred Texts: The Guru Granth Sahib and Sikhism. Anita Ganeri, (Evans, 2002)

The Atlas of World Religions. Anita Ganeri, (Franklin Watts, 2002)

The Lion Encyclopedia of Christianity. David Self, (Lion Hudson, 2007)

The Usborne Encyclopedia of Major World Religions. Susan Meredith and Clare Hickman, (Usborne, 2005)

World Faiths: Judaism. Trevor Barnes, (Kingfisher, 2005)

World Religions Today: Buddhism/Christianity. Kathryn Walker, (Wayland, 2007)

World Religions Today: Hinduism/Judaism/Islam. Gianna Quaglia, (Wayland, 2007)

Websites

These websites offer comprehensive information about the six major world religions, plus many other faiths. In addition, each has links to numerous individual faith websites.

www.bbc.co.uk/religion/religions

http://bible.beliefnet.com/index.html

www.religionfacts.com

This website has helpful information about rites of passage:

http://encarta.msn.com/encyclopedia_76155 7678_1____2/Rites_of_Passage.html#s2

TEACHER NOTES

- Ask an elderly relative, neighbour or family friend how he or she celebrated their coming of age. How and when would you like to mark your own coming of age? How does this differ from what your grandparents did?

- Make a list of several countries, each in different continents. Find out the legal ages at which young people there are allowed to marry, to drive and to vote.

- Arrange for an imam, a rabbi, a priest, a member of the khalsa, a Buddhist monk or nun or a Hindu priest to visit your school. Ask them how they mark coming of age in their religion.

- Ask the local council for a list of local Buddhist monasteries, Hindu temples, Islamic mosques, Sikh gurdwaras and Jewish synagogues. Arrange to visit one of them.

Index